W9-ARA-357

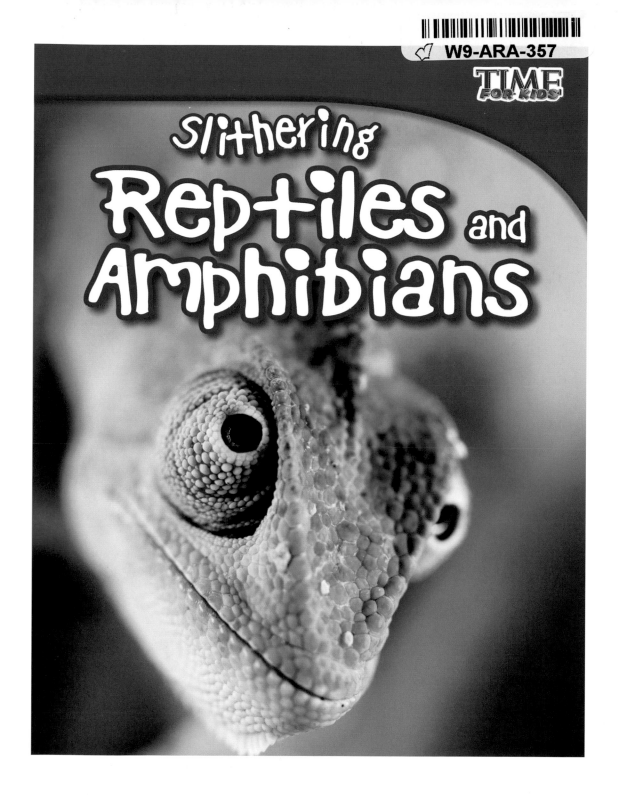

slithering Reptiles and Amphibians

Debra J. Housel

Consultants

Timothy Rasinski, Ph.D.
Kent State University
Bill Houska, D.V.M.
James K. Morrisey, D.V.M.

Publishing Credits

Dona Herweck Rice, *Editor-in-Chief*
Robin Erickson, *Production Director*
Lee Aucoin, *Creative Director*
Conni Medina, M.A.Ed., *Editorial Director*
Jamey Acosta, *Editor*
Heidi Kellenberger, *Editor*
Lexa Hoang, *Designer*
Leslie Palmer, *Designer*
Stephanie Reid, *Photo Editor*
Rachelle Cracchiolo, M.S.Ed., *Publisher*

Image Credits

Cover Sebastian Duda/Shutterstock; worldswildlifewonders/Shutterstock; p.4 EcoPrint/ Shutterstock; p.4-5 back: Eric Isselée/Shutterstock; p.4-5 inset: Eric Isselée/Shutterstock; p.5 dedek/Shutterstock; p.6 Cameramannz/Shutterstock; p.6 inset: Eric Isselée/Shutterstock; p.6-9, 18-19 back: Eric Isselée/Shutterstock; p.7 Lucian Coman/Shutterstock; p.8 Tom McHugh/ Photo Researchers; p.9 Hans Pfletschinger/Photo Library; p.10 mmedia/Big Stock Photo; p.10-11 back: Gladskikh Tatiana/Shutterstock; p.11 top: Trevor kelly/Shutterstock; p.11 bottom: Philippe Henry/Photo Library; p.12 John Warburton-Lee Photography/Alamy; p.12-13 back: Eric Isselée/ Shutterstock; p.13 top: iphotoworld/iStockphoto; p.13 bottom: Tony Allen/Photo Library; p.14 top: MonicaOttino/Shutterstock; p.14 bottom: kkaplin/Shutterstock; p.15 Cathy Keifer/Shutterstock; p.16 top: Jurie Maree/Shutterstock; p.16 bottom: Rudy Umans/Shutterstock; p.16-17 back: Joy Brown/Shutterstock; p.17 top: Natali Glado/Shutterstock; p.17 inset: fivespots/Shutterstock; p.17 bottom: Elizabeth Spencer/Shutterstock; p.18 Minden Pictures RM/Getty Images; p.19 top: sarah2/ Shutterstock; p.19 left: Paul Broadbent/Shutterstock; p.19 right: LesPalenik/Shutterstock; p.20 inset top: Pan Xunbin/Shutterstock; p.20 inset center: Davit Buachidze/Shutterstock; p.20 inset bottom: Educational Images LTD/Custom Medical Stock Photo CMSP Biology/Newscom; p.20 bottom: Kyodo/Newscom; p.20-21 Eric Isselée/Shutterstock; p.21 top: Joel Sartore/Getty Images; p.22-23 back: Dr. Morley Read/Shutterstock; p.23 inset: Cathy Keifer/Shutterstock; p.23 Rick Neese; p.24 worldswildlifewonders/Shutterstock; p.24-25 Eric Isselée/Shutterstock; p.25 Chris Mattison/ Alamy; p.26 left: worldswildlifewonders/Shutterstock; p.26 right: alslutsky/Shutterstock; p.26 back: G-ZStudio/Shutterstock; back cover: fivespot/ Shutterstock

Based on writing from *TIME For Kids*.
TIME For Kids and the *TIME For Kids* logo are registered trademarks of TIME Inc.
Used under license.

Teacher Created Materials

5301 Oceanus Drive
Huntington Beach, CA 92649-1030
http://www.tcmpub.com
ISBN 978-1-4333-3659-1
© 2012 Teacher Created Materials, Inc.

Table of Contents

What Is a Reptile?

Have you seen a **snake** or a **lizard** lying in the sun? Why do they do that? They are **reptiles**, and they need the heat that comes from the sun.

Reptiles need heat from their **environments** to **maintain** their body temperatures. Unlike you, reptiles are **cold-blooded** animals.

▼ There are more than 6,500 kinds of reptiles. Tortoises are one of them.

leopard tortoise

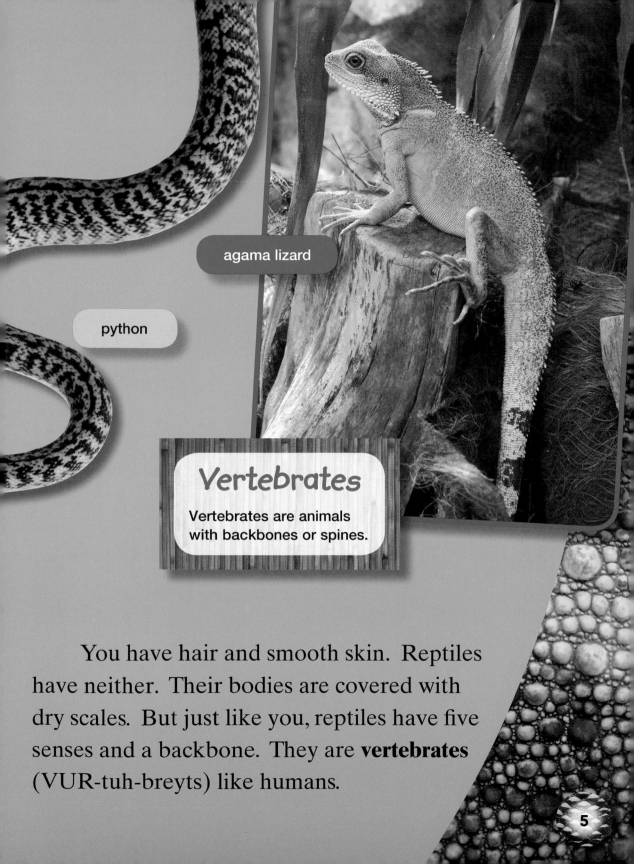

agama lizard

python

Vertebrates

Vertebrates are animals with backbones or spines.

You have hair and smooth skin. Reptiles have neither. Their bodies are covered with dry scales. But just like you, reptiles have five senses and a backbone. They are **vertebrates** (VUR-tuh-breyts) like humans.

Kinds of Reptiles

There are four reptile groups.

The first group includes lizards and reptiles. Lizards live in warm places. Most lizards avoid water, but marine iguanas swim in the sea. Snakes have spines that bend and twist to let them move. They also have sharp teeth, and some have fangs. From the desert to the sea, snakes are found in many different environments.

Crocodilians have short, stubby **limbs**. Both crocodiles and alligators live in and near warm water.

Third Eye

The tuatara has a third eye on top of its head! The eye can only see light and dark.

◄ Tuataras only live on islands off the coast of New Zealand.

The desert tortoise lives where it is hot and dry.

Be Careful!

Some people keep reptiles as pets. If you touch reptiles, always wash your hands afterward. They may have **salmonella** (sal-muh-NEL-uh) on their scales. Salmonella is a germ. It doesn't hurt the reptiles, but it could make you very sick.

Turtles and **tortoises** have shells. When one gets attacked, it pulls its head, limbs, and tail inside. Unless the predator can crack its shell, the turtle or tortoise stays safe. Tortoises usually live on land. Turtles live in or near water. They are good swimmers. Some even live in the sea.

Tuataras (too-uh-TAHR-uhs) are the fourth reptile group. They look like lizards, but they are more closely related to dinosaurs than any other reptiles.

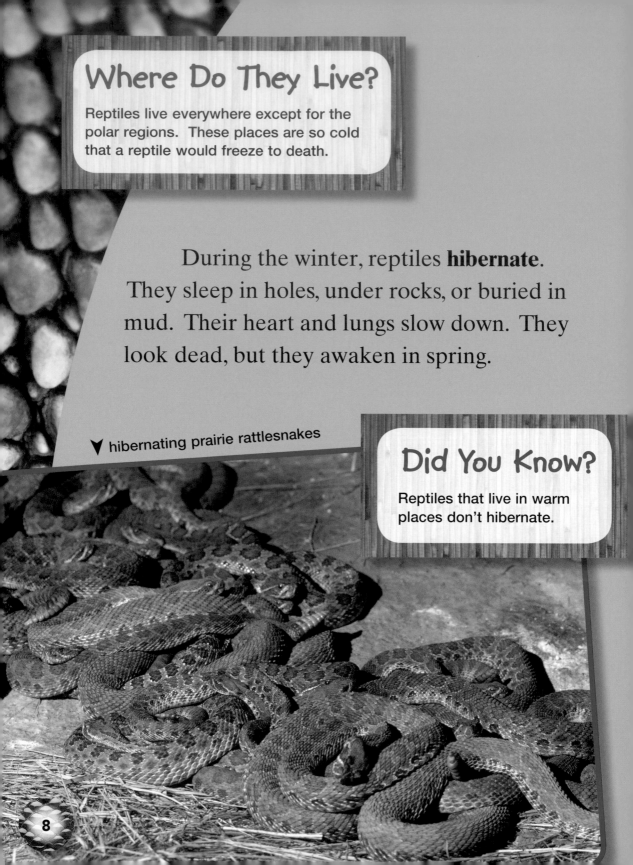

Where Do They Live?

Reptiles live everywhere except for the polar regions. These places are so cold that a reptile would freeze to death.

During the winter, reptiles **hibernate**. They sleep in holes, under rocks, or buried in mud. Their heart and lungs slow down. They look dead, but they awaken in spring.

▼ hibernating prairie rattlesnakes

Did You Know?

Reptiles that live in warm places don't hibernate.

▼ New skin may grow beneath the old skin.

A New Snake?

Long ago people believed that snakes lived forever. People thought snakes were reborn when they shed their skins.

Lizards and snakes shed their skin. A lizard's skin flakes off. A snake's skin peels off in one piece.

Some snakes and lizards give birth to live young, but most reptiles lay eggs. They dig a hole in soil, bury their eggs, and leave.

▼ turtle eggs hatching

Boy or Girl?

For some baby turtles, the temperature of the soil in the nest determines whether they will be male or female. In the coldest parts of the nest, female turtles hatch. Male turtles hatch in the parts of the nest that are warmer.

▲ crocodile eggs hatching

After the babies hatch, female alligators may carry them around for up to one year. ➤

Only a few reptiles care for their young, but a female crocodile stays near her nest. When the babies hatch, she picks up each one with her jaws. She carries it to the water. Alligators guard their nests, too.

Snakes are **carnivores** (KAHR-nuh-vohrs) because they eat meat. A python wraps around an animal and squeezes it so hard that the animal cannot breathe.

Some snakes have **venom**, or poison. They bite **prey** with their fangs. Poison flows through the fangs and kills the animal.

▼ A python squeezes its prey so it cannot breathe.

Supersize

Snakes swallow animals whole. A snake can unhinge its jaws so that it can swallow things five times its size. That's like you swallowing your front door!

▲ Some snakes have fangs with poison.

Lizards

If an animal grabs the tail of some kinds of lizards, the lizard can lose its tail and run away. It may even slowly regrow a new tail!

▼ The Komodo dragon delivers a nasty bite with its sharp teeth. The bacteria in its saliva slowly poisons the animal over the course of several days.

A Full Stomach

If an alligator eats a big animal, it may not eat again for three months!

▲ Chameleons can change color
to blend into their environment.

Reptiles do not chew their food. Some reptiles tear prey into big chunks before swallowing. Snapping turtles bite small prey in half with their sharp beaks and strong jaws. Even plant eaters, or **herbivores**, don't chew. They use their teeth to tear off leaves and stems.

Reptiles must protect themselves from **predators**. When attacked, some snakes play dead by flipping over. Some lizards use **camouflage** (KAM-uh-flahzh). They blend into their surroundings by turning shades of brown, yellow, or green.

Reptile Life Spans

Reptiles can live for different lengths of time. Most members of the **species** (SPEE-sheez) die by the age shown below. A few live longer.

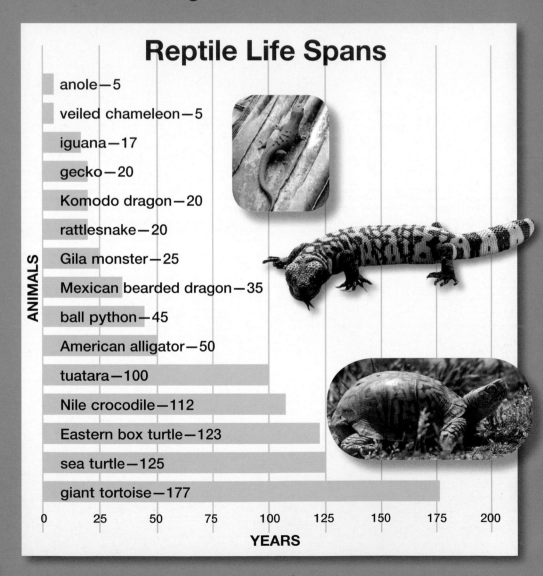

Reptile Life Spans

ANIMALS

- anole—5
- veiled chameleon—5
- iguana—17
- gecko—20
- Komodo dragon—20
- rattlesnake—20
- Gila monster—25
- Mexican bearded dragon—35
- ball python—45
- American alligator—50
- tuatara—100
- Nile crocodile—112
- Eastern box turtle—123
- sea turtle—125
- giant tortoise—177

0   25   50   75   100   125   150   175   200

YEARS

sea turtle

▲ The American alligator is a common sight in the Florida Everglades.

What Is an Amphibian?

Amphibians are also cold-blooded vertebrates. How do they differ from reptiles? They must keep their skin moist. They never take a drink. They **absorb** water and oxygen through their skin.

Most amphibians live in or near freshwater. Amphibians with limbs have **webbed** feet to help them swim. If they live in places with harsh winters, they hibernate as reptiles do.

World's Biggest Frog

The world's biggest frog is the goliath frog of West Africa. It can grow up to 14 inches (35 cm) long and weigh over 6 pounds (3 kg). Its eyes are the same size as yours!

Amphibians were the first vertebrates to live on land. ▲

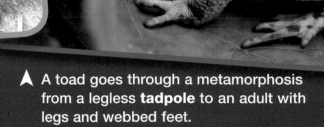

▲ A toad goes through a metamorphosis from a legless **tadpole** to an adult with legs and webbed feet.

Most amphibians change after birth. This is called **metamorphosis** (MET-uh-MOHR-fuh-sis). Metamorphosis means to change from one form to another. For example, frogs and toads don't begin life with webbed feet. In fact, they don't even have legs at first!

Kinds of Amphibians

▼ Amphibians belong to one of three groups. Take a look.

With Tails	newts, olms, salamanders	
Without Tails	frogs, toads	
No Legs	caecilians	

Giant Salamanders

Chinese and Japanese giant salamanders are the biggest amphibians. They can be longer than you are tall and weigh as much as 88 pounds! They can live 50 years, but people kill them for food. That is why they are **endangered**.

Salamanders, **newts**, and **olms** are amphibians with tails. If they lose a leg or tail, they may regrow it. Like frogs and toads, they change through metamorphosis. Most salamanders begin life as **larvae** in a pond. Some salamanders lay eggs on land. When those babies hatch, they look like tiny adult salamanders.

red spotted newt

Newts and salamanders stay under rocks and rarely come out. Olms live in watery caves. They look like eels with four tiny limbs. They develop lungs without losing their **gills**.

Although they start life with tails, adult frogs and toads have none. They form the second group of amphibians.

Frogs and toads begin life as eggs. Once the eggs are laid, the parents swim away. Most frogs and toads do not raise their young.

A few weeks later tiny tadpoles appear from the eggs. Tadpoles have gills. They breathe underwater like fish. They stay in shallow water, eating small water bugs.

Over a few weeks, the tadpoles change. They grow legs, and their gills shrink. Their tails are slowly absorbed into their bodies. They start breathing with lungs. They can no longer breathe underwater. They must come to the surface or drown. Baby frogs spend much of their time in the water, but tiny toads leave to live on land.

More About Toads

Baby toads are the size of insects. Since adult toads eat bugs, you might think they might eat their own babies. But that does not happen. Toads have a glow on their skin that other toads can see. Adult toads somehow know not to eat things that glow.

Toad or Frog?

How can you tell toads and frogs apart? Toads have dry, bumpy skin. Frogs have smooth, shiny skin.

A Toad's Life Cycle

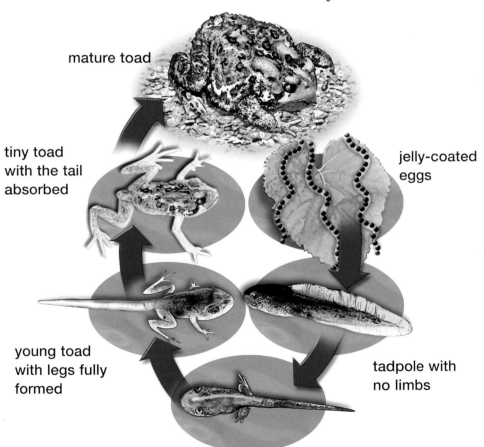

mature toad

tiny toad with the tail absorbed

jelly-coated eggs

young toad with legs fully formed

tadpole with no limbs

tadpole with small legs

If they survive the summer, toads hibernate. While a toad sleeps during its first winter, it gets bumps on its skin. The bumps fill with a fluid. The fluid has a bad taste, so it helps to protect the toads. Most animals spit out a toad when they taste it. People call it *toad poison*, but it's harmless.

Some frogs do have poison. The colorful poison dart frog lives in South America. It has deadly venom in its skin.

▲ Wild poison dart frogs have poisonous skin.

Caecilians are the third amphibian group. Scientists don't know much about them. They live underground in the warm, moist tropics. They have no legs, and they look like large worms. Although they have eyes, they cannot see very well.

It is very rare to see caecilians like this one. ➤

A Good Pet?

Some people keep poison dart frogs as pets! That may sound unsafe, but it isn't always. The frogs develop the powerful poison because of the beetles they eat in the wild. If the frogs are not in the wild to eat the beetles, they don't develop the poison.

What do you think it is like to live underground? To bury yourself deep into the mud? What is it like to live underwater, to have scales, or slither on the ground? Ask a reptile or an amphibian. They'll know!

panther chameleon

red-eyed tree frog

Glossary

absorb—to take in through the skin

amphibians—cold-blooded vertebrates that have moist skin

caecilians—worm-like amphibians that live their entire lives underground

camouflage—an animal's body feature that helps it to hide from its enemies

carnivores—animals that eat only meat

cold-blooded—having blood that stays at about the same temperature as the water or air around the living thing

crocodilians—large meat-eating reptiles that live near water in warm, moist, tropical regions, includes crocodiles and alligators

endangered—at risk of dying out completely

environments—surrounding areas

gills—slits near the head that allow animals to breathe oxygen underwater

herbivores—animals that eat only plants

hibernate—to spend the winter in a resting state

larvae—the early forms of some amphibians before they change into their adult shape

limbs—the body parts that stick out from an animal's main body such as arms and legs

lizard—a reptile that lives in warm regions and usually has four limbs

maintain—to stay the same

metamorphosis—a big and noticeable change in how something looks, what it does, what it is made of, or how it is made

newts—tiny salamanders that spend their entire lives in the water

olms—amphibians that have both gills and lungs, tiny limbs, and tails

predators—animals that hunt, kill, and eat other animals

prey—any animal that is hunted, killed, and eaten by another animal

reptiles—cold-blooded vertebrates that have skin covered with scales

salamanders—amphibians that look like lizards but have smooth, moist skin

salmonella—a germ which can cause sickness in humans and is sometimes found on reptiles

snake—a reptile without limbs that moves by using its flexible spine

species—a group of animals or plants that are like one another

tadpole—an infant toad or frog having a head, gills, and tail that can live only in water

tortoises—reptiles that have shells and usually live on land

tuataras—lizard-like reptiles closely related to dinosaurs

turtles—reptiles that have shells and usually live in or near water

venom—poison passed from a snake's fangs (sharp, pointed teeth) to its prey

vertebrates—animals that have spines (backbones)

webbed—having toes joined by a thin piece of skin

Index